MEXICO
BEAUTIFUL LAND
DIVERSE PEOPLE

THE PACIFIC SOUTH STATES OF MEXICO

SHERYL NANTUS

Gulf of
Mexico

24°N

22°N

MEXICO

Bay of Campeche

20°N

Colima

COLIMA

18°N

GUERRERO

CHIAPAS

Chilpancingo

Oaxaca

Tuxtla Gutiérrez

Acapulco

OAXACA

16°N

Gulf of
Tehuantepec

GUATEMALA

N

W   E

S

14°N

PACIFIC OCEAN

12°N

0   100   200 Miles

0   100   200 Kilometers

Albers Conic Equal-Area Projection

10°N

104°W   102°W   100°W   98°W   96°W   94°W   92°W

MEXICO
BEAUTIFUL LAND
DIVERSE PEOPLE

THE PACIFIC SOUTH STATES OF MEXICO

SHERYL NANTUS

Mason Crest Publishers
Philadelphia

Mason Crest Publishers
370 Reed Road
Broomall PA 19008
www.masoncrest.com

First printing

1 3 5 7 9 8 6 4 2

Library of Congress Cataloging-in-Publication Data

Nantus, Sheryl.
   The Pacific south states of Mexico / Sheryl Nantus.
       p. cm. — (Mexico--beautiful land, diverse people)
   Includes index.
   ISBN 978-1-4222-0666-9 (hardcover) — ISBN 978-1-4222-0733-8 (pbk.)
   1. Mexico—Juvenile literature. 2. Pacific Coast (Mexico)-—Juvenile literature. [1. Pacific
Coast (Mexico) 2. Mexico.] I. Title.
   F1208.5.N36 2008
   972—dc22
                                        2008031869

TABLE OF CONTENTS

MEXICO
BEAUTIFUL LAND
DIVERSE PEOPLE

INTRODUCTION

Mexico is a country in the midst of great change. And what happens in Mexico reverberates in the United States, its neighbor to the north.

For outsiders, the most obvious of Mexico's recent changes has occurred in the political realm. From 1929 until the end of the 20th century, the country was ruled by a single political party: the Partido Revolucionario Institucional, or PRI (in English, the Institutional Revolutionary Party). Over the years, PRI governments became notorious for corruption, and the Mexican economy languished. In 2000, however, the PRI's stranglehold on national politics was broken with the election of Vicente Fox as Mexico's president. Fox, of the Partido de Acción Nacional (National Action Party), or PAN, promised political reform and economic development but had a mixed record as president. However, another PAN candidate, Felipe Calderón, succeeded Fox in 2006 after a hotly contested and highly controversial election. That election saw Calderón win by the slimmest of margins over a candidate from the Partido de la Revolución Democrática (Party of the Democratic Revolution). The days of one-party rule in Mexico, it seems, are gone for good.

Mexico's economy, like its politics, has seen significant changes in recent years. A 1994 free-trade agreement with the United States and Canada, along with the increasing transfer of industries from government control to private ownership under President Fox and President Calderón, has helped spur economic growth in Mexico. When all the world's countries are compared,

Mexico now falls into the upper-middle range in per-capita income. This means that, on average, Mexicans enjoy a higher standard of living than people in the majority of the world's countries. Yet averages can be misleading. In Mexico there is an enormous gap between haves and have-nots. According to some estimates, 40 percent of the country's more than 100 million people live in poverty. In some areas of Mexico, particularly in rural villages, jobs are almost nonexistent. This has driven millions of Mexicans to immigrate to the United States (with or without proper documentation) in search of a better life.

By 2006 more than 11 million people born in Mexico were living in the United States (including more than 6 million illegal immigrants), according to estimates based on data from the Pew Hispanic Center and the U.S. Census Bureau. Meanwhile, nearly one of every 10 people living in the United States was of Mexican ancestry. Clearly, Mexico and Mexicans have had—and will continue to have—a major influence on American society.

It is especially unfortunate, then, that many American students know little about their country's neighbor to the south. The books in the MEXICO: BEAUTIFUL LAND, DIVERSE PEOPLE series are designed to help correct that.

As readers will discover, Mexico boasts a rich, vibrant culture that is a blend of indigenous and European—especially Spanish—influences. More than 3,000 years ago, the Olmec people created a complex society and built imposing monuments that survive to this day in the Mexican states of Tabasco and Veracruz. In the fifth century A.D., when the Roman Empire collapsed and Europe entered its so-called Dark Age, the Mayan civilization was already flourishing in the jungles of the Yucatán Peninsula—and it would enjoy another four centuries of tremendous cultural achievements. By the time the Spanish conqueror Hernán Cortés landed at Veracruz in 1519, another great indigenous civilization, the Aztecs, had emerged to dominate much of Mexico.

With a force of about 500 soldiers, plus a few horses and cannons, Cortés marched inland toward the Aztec capital, Tenochtitlán. Built in the middle of a lake in what is now Mexico City, Tenochtitlán was an engineering marvel and one of the largest cities anywhere in the world at the time. With allies from among the indigenous peoples who resented being ruled by the Aztecs—and aided by a smallpox epidemic—Cortés and the Spaniards managed to conquer the Aztec Empire in 1521 after a brutal fight that devastated Tenochtitlán.

It was in that destruction that modern Mexico was born. Spaniards married indigenous people, creating mestizo offspring—as well as a distinctive Mexican culture that was neither Spanish nor indigenous but combined elements of both.

Spain ruled Mexico for three centuries. After an unsuccessful revolution in 1810, Mexico finally won its independence in 1821.

But the newly born country continued to face many difficulties. Among them were bad rulers, beginning with a military officer named Agustín Iturbide, who had himself crowned emperor only a year after Mexico threw off the yoke of Spain. In 1848 Mexico lost a war with the United States—and was forced to give up almost half of its territory as a result. During the 1860s French forces invaded Mexico and installed a puppet emperor. While Mexico regained its independence in 1867 under national hero Benito Juárez, the long dictatorship of Porfirio Díaz would soon follow.

Díaz was overthrown in a revolution that began in 1910, but Mexico would be racked by fighting until the Partido Revolucionario Institucional took over in 1929. The PRI brought stability and economic progress, but its rule became increasingly corrupt.

Today, with the PRI's long monopoly on power swept away, Mexico stands on the brink of a new era. Difficult problems such as entrenched inequalities and grinding poverty remain. But progress toward a more open political system may lead to economic and social progress as well. Mexico—a land with a rich and ancient heritage—may emerge as one of the 21st century's most inspiring success stories.

1

THE LAND

Mexico's Pacific South is a land rich in history and natural resources. These states—Colima, Guerrero, Oaxaca, Chiapas—are a diverse mixture of mountains and tropical vegetation. They are sometimes shaken by earthquakes and volcanoes, or tossed and flooded by hurricanes, but their beauty remains.

Colima is one of the smallest states in Mexico, with only 2,106 square miles (5,455 square kilometers) in total, only 0.3 percent of Mexico's total land. But this small area has a great variety of environments within it, from warm and humid temperatures at an average 78 degrees Fahrenheit (26 degrees Celsius) in the Armería River valley near the center of the state, to a brisker 62 degrees Fahrenheit (17 degrees Celsius) in the higher altitudes to the northwest. The coast of Colima is at the latitude of 19 degrees north, the same as Jamaica and Hawaii.

Between December and February you can find the coolest temperatures for this area, although nothing like the North American winter. The weather is warm for most of the rest of the year, with the

There is beautiful scenery throughout mountainous Chiapas, including the steep walls of the Canyon de Sumidero in Tuxtla Gutiérrez.

rainy season running between June and October; providing needed moisture to the forest after the hot and humid months of July and August. Unfortunately, the rainy season is also the hurricane season, a major concern for many. While Colima was badly hit by Hurricane Pauline in October of 1997, the nearby states of Guerrero and Oaxaca were hit much harder, with over 200 deaths and major destruction of property.

Colima is surrounded on three sides by Jalisco and by Michoacán to the southeast. Directly south of Colima is the Pacific Ocean, where the Revillagigedo Archipelago lies, part of Colima as well. Although it is one of the smallest states in Mexico, Colima has some of the most varied geographical features. Starting at the many beaches on the Pacific Coast, the land rises up to the rich farms that dot the countryside. At the northeastern tip of the state, two volcanoes tower over the small villages—and one of them is still quite active!

Sitting right at the southernmost edge of Mexico is Chiapas, the eighth largest state in the country. Consisting of 28,732 square miles (74,416 square kilometers), its boundaries run along the Pacific Ocean to the south to the border with Guatemala in the east and then north to the state of Tabasco, with Oaxaca and Veracruz bordering it to the west.

Going inward from the coast, you immediately find yourself climbing the Sierra Madre de Chiapas, a large mountain range running parallel to the ocean. These mountains reach up to 13,310 feet (4,057 meters), with the spectacular Tacaná Volcano just inside the Guatemala border. Moving inland, you find the lush river valley of the Grijalva and northeast of them the central highlands, with lower lakes and valleys feeding into the Usumacinta River and eventually into Tabasco. Most of

Mayan boys swim through the streets after Hurricane Roxanne flooded their town in 1995. Hurricanes and tropical storms are always a danger in the Pacific south states of Mexico.

the forest is made up of valuable **dyewoods** and hardwoods, making it both an economic and cultural treasure, as more and more discussion arises about how to both preserve the forests and harvest the benefits of the land for the people. Two of the most popular woods harvested here are **mahogany** and **rosewood**.

The climate of Chiapas varies from area to area. In the north part of the state you can find very dry hot weather, varying greatly from the southern parts where the humidity makes the air feel hotter than the actual temperature. The average temperature is 68 degrees Fahrenheit (20 degrees Celsius), with some measurements going as high as 104 degrees Fahrenheit (40 degrees Celsius) and as low as 32 degrees Fahrenheit (0 degrees Celsius). The rainy season runs from June to November. Needless to say, if you visit Chiapas, you'll need to prepare for all types of weather.

Located on the Pacific Coast, Guerrero has one of Mexico's most famous cities in its midst—Acapulco. With a surface area of 24,818 miles (64,282 square kilometers), this state has only 3.3 percent of Mexico's land area, but that includes 313 miles (500 kilometers) of coastline. The Sierra Madre del Sur runs southwest just inside the coastline, cresting at 12,149 feet (3,703 meters). Bordered to the north and west by Michoacán; Oaxaca to the east and southeast; Puebla to the northeast; and Morelos to the northwest, Guerrero occupies a small but important position in Mexico past and present.

The main river running through the area is called the Río de las Balsas, beginning at the northwest tip of the state and running almost directly down the center, with smaller rivers branching off until it meets Oaxaca at the other end of the state. Because of the moisture available

The western Sierra Madre mountain range, which runs through Chiapas, Guerrero, and Oaxaca, features a great variety of lush vegetation.

A plume of ash rises from the top of a volcano that erupted in 1991 near the border between Colima and Jalisco.

and the temperatures that can vary from a high of over 90 degrees Fahrenheit (32 degrees Celsius) to a low of 80 degrees Fahrenheit (26 degrees Celsius), the climate is hot and rainy on the coastlines. On the highlands further inland, near the center of the Mexican peninsula, the climate balances out enough so crops can be grown and harvested.

Oaxaca is found in the southwest area of Mexico, with the Pacific Ocean to the south. It shares borders with Guerrero, Chiapas, Puebla, and Veracruz. With a surface area of 94,211 square miles (244,007 square kilometers), Oaxaca is one of the five largest states of Mexico,

A church partially buried by the eruption of Paricutín, a volcano in the region. The States of Mexico's Pacific coast are part of the "ring of fire," a circle of active volcanoes.

with 4.85 percent of the nation's total surface area. Sitting along the mountains and valleys of the Tehuantepec Isthmus, this large state has a tropical climate resulting in massive amounts of rainfall throughout the land. Almost totally encircled by the Sierra Madre del Sur mountain range, the Oaxaca *plateau* contains extremely fertile land and is well suited to farming and agriculture. It produces sugarcane, coffee, and tobacco, among other crops.

The Isthmus of Tehuantepec is the name given to the narrowest piece of land in North America—as you can see on a map, it is extremely narrow and just barely separates the Pacific and Atlantic Oceans. Historically, this was an invaluable resource to travelers looking to avoid going all the way around the tip of South America; it was eagerly sought by traders and explorers alike.

With almost 316 miles (500 kilometers) of coastline, Oaxaca is poised to become a major tourist-based state, like its other nearby sister states. Until recently the beaches were ignored, but thanks to a series of government initiatives, such places as the Bahias de Huatulco project are appearing on tourist maps and destinations.

COLIMA

Location: Colima is surrounded on three sides by Jalisco and by Michoacán to the southeast. Directly south of Colima is the Pacific Ocean, where the Revillagigedo Archipelago lies, which is part of Colima as well.

Capital: Colima

Total Area: 2,106 square miles (5,455 square kilometers) in total; 103 miles (166 kilometers) of coastline.

Climate: Warm and humid with an average temperature of 78 degrees Fahrenheit (26 degrees Celsius).

Terrain: Nearly three quarters of Colima consists of mountains and hills.

Elevation: Fuego de Colima rises into the sky at 14,220 feet (4,323 meters) and Volcán de Fuego is 13,087 feet (3,980 meters) of live, active volcano.

Natural Hazards: Volcanoes; hurricanes.

CHIAPAS

Location: Sitting right at the southernmost edge of Mexico is Chiapas, the eighth largest state in the country. Its boundaries run along the Pacific Ocean to the south to the border with Guatemala in the east and then north to the state of Tabasco, with Oaxaca and Veracruz bordering it to the west.

Capital: Tuxtla Gutiérrez

Total Area: 28,732 square miles (74,416 square kilometers), with over 173 miles (280 kilometers) of coastline.

Climate: The average temperature is 68 degrees Fahrenheit (20 degrees Celsius) with some measurements going as high as 104 degrees Fahrenheit (40 degrees Celsius) and as low as 32 degrees Fahrenheit (0 degrees Celsius). The rainy season runs from June to November.

Terrain: Going inward from the coast, you immediately find yourself climbing the Sierra Madre de Chiapas, a large mountain range running parallel to the ocean.

Elevation: The highest point in Chiapas is 13,310 feet (4,057 meters) at the Sierra Madre de Chiapas, with the lowest points being at sea level along the coastline.

Natural Hazards: Flooding.

GUERRERO

Location: Sitting on the Pacific Coast to the south of Michoacán and bordered by Oaxaca ot the east and southeast and Puebla to the northeast, with Morelos to the northwest.

Capital: Chilpancingo

Total Area: 24,887 square miles (64,457 square kilometers)

Climate: Hot and rainy with temperatures ranging from 79 degrees Fahrenheit (26 degrees Celsius) on the coast to a cooler 59 degrees Fahrenheit (15 degrees Celsius) in the highlands where the land is drier and easier to farm.

Terrain: Mountainous throughout the state except for along the coastline.

Elevation: Rising from sea level on the coastline, the Sierra Madre del Sur reaches heights of well over 12,000 feet (3,000 meters) with notable mountains being Cerro de la Cruz at 7,250 feet (2,210 meters) and Cerro Baúl at 10,215 feet (3,114 meters).

Natural Hazards: Hurricanes and earthquakes.

OAXACA

Location: Just north of the state of Chiapas, Oaxaca lies on the Pacific Ocean with the state of Veracruz to the north.

Capital: Oaxaca

Total Area: 36,375 square miles (94,211 square kilometers)

Climate: Tropical in the interior; hot and dry on the coast. Average temperatures are approximately 84 degrees Fahrenheit (29 degrees Celsius).

Terrain: Valleys dominate in the southern area with plateaus rising in the north to provide fertile farmland.

Elevation: The Sierra de Oaxaca has peaks as high as 10,000 feet.

Natural Hazards: Earthquakes.

19

An ancient stone temple stands in Palenque, Chiapas. Mayan remains such as this can be seen throughout the region.

2

THE HISTORY

Before the coming of the Spanish, Colima first came into its own as the Tecos Indians solidified their hold on the area. When they conquered the local area, they ensured that the kingdom of Colima became one of the most important parts of the ancient Chimalhuacana Confederation. But as the Spanish *conquistadors* swept across the country, Colima soon became a part of their new empire; the capital city of Colima was founded in 1523 by Gonzalo de Sandoval. Cortés, the famous explorer and conquistador, even appointed his nephew mayor of the city a few years later, hoping that the seaport would make Colima a valuable *asset* to the Spanish throne. But the Spanish king decided that Acapulco would make a better seaport and left Colima alone. As time went on, more and more land was added to Colima, resulting in a larger coastal presence. It became more important to the travelers going up and down the coastline, seeking safe harbors and trading posts. President Porfirio Díaz built a railroad across the small state to the new city of Manzanillo in the 1800s, making it a vital port of call for many ships.

In the early 20th century, during the Mexican Revolution, Colima suffered greatly, changing hands as the battles raged back and forth across its fertile lands. Slowly, though, the mining and shipping industries grew—and then the tourism industry grew and prospered as travelers discovered the beautiful beaches and allure of the still-active volcano.

The name comes from the Nahuatl language of the Aztecs, and it meant "old kingdom" or "domain of the lord." Literally, Colima was the "place conquered by our grandfathers"—or the "place dominated or ruled by the Fire God," a reference to the volcanoes nearby on the border between Colima and Jalisco.

The name Chiapas actually comes from two Nahuatl words, "Chia" and "Apan," meaning "in the river." Many people have lived in this area for as far back as there is recorded history, among them the Maya and the Aztecs. Many Mayan ruins dot the countryside, providing a great opportunity for archeologists to study this lost civilization. Many of these cities include pyramids, as well as drainage systems, huge statues, and intricate artwork centuries ahead of other civilizations at that time in Europe.

But the arrival of the Spanish in the 1500s meant the death of this civilization as the conquistadors raged across the countryside, plundering and attacking the inhabitants as well as introducing deadly diseases such as *smallpox* into the environment. The Maya had already begun to move away from their large cities, dispersing into small villages in the region, and the Spanish took very little note of them as they ransacked the area, searching for gold and precious metals. As the invaders set up their local governments, they left most native people

The Spanish conquistador Hernán Cortés meets the Aztec emperor Montezuma in this 19th-century illustration. The arrival of the Spaniards in the early 16th century forever changed life in Mexico.

alone and concentrated on collecting taxes and creating plantations to grow coffee and sugar. However, the Spanish experienced a high rate of failure in this region, due to the *malaria* and other diseases in the area that drained their labor force. Many Maya kept away from the Spanish, keeping to their small villages and creating their own societies where interaction with their invaders was kept to a minimum.

At this time, Chiapas was recognized as a province of Guatemala, not Mexico. Lacking the natural resources of the other areas to the north, Chiapas became a strategic worry for Spain as it tried to keep its hold

El Nevado, the "volcano of fire," is located on the border of Colima. The state got its name from the many volcanoes in the region.

on its conquests in the midst of losing its other territories. Attempts at farming continued, with the Indians being forced into labor under Spanish rule. This led to constant conflict between the Native Americans and the Spanish as each side tried to gain the upper hand.

Mexico, Guatemala, and the rest of the Spanish-conquered territories gained their independence in 1821. For another two years, Chiapas remained the property of Guatemala. Then, the citizens voted to join Mexico on September 14, 1824. This date is still celebrated all over Chiapas as the Día de la Mexicanidad or Day of Mexicanization. In 1892, the capital of Chiapas was moved from San Cristóbal to Tuxtla Gutiérrez.

Unfortunately, in the last decade violence has marred the face of Chiapas. In 1994, several towns were occupied by rebels who wanted more independence for all of Mexico's native communities. Computer hackers have gotten involved with the Zapatista rebels also, sabotaging Mexican government sites since 1998 and attempting to overload the servers. Under Vicente Fox's new government, elected in 2000, communication between the rebels and President Fox's officials improved, leading to increased hope of a peaceful resolution for all parties involved.

During Fox's 2000-2006 presidency, he repeatedly expressed the hope of ending the violence in Chiapas through compromise and negotiation. Soon after he took office, he began passing legislation to make life easier for the indigenous of Chiapas. He also talked to Zapatista leaders and ordered the release of some of the group's jailed members. However, the Fox administration did not completely reconcile the conflicts. Once Fox completed his term as President, it was uncertain how his successor, Felipe Calderón, would handle the forces of rebellion in Chiapas.

Like much of Mexico, Guerrero was the site of many ancient civilizations, with much activity concentrated on the coast. One such place was Zihuatanejo, not far from Ixtapa. Archeological digs in this area

The original natives of Oaxaca included the Miztec, who built this compound hundreds of years ago.

This carved mask depicts a Mayan fire god. The Mayan civilization was in decline by the time the Spanish arrived in the 16th century, but descendants of the Mayans still live throughout the country today.

discovered stone carvings and figurines dating as far back as 3000 B.C., when the Olmecs were known to be in the area.

Like most other areas conquered by the Spanish, Guerrero suffered under the rule of the invaders for centuries, while being exploited as a source of natural resources. Its valuable seaports offered easy access to the wealth of the Mexican interior.

Unfortunately, this area was also the site of some of the heaviest fighting in the Mexican war for independence, weakening the local *infrastructure* even more in the early 1800s. Even after the Spanish disappeared from the scene, the state known as Guerrero did not exist until 1849; the land was divided up between the states of Michoacán, Puebla, and Oaxaca. But pressure from the local inhabitants who wanted control over their own land and an urge to remember Vicente

Guerrero, the president who put an end to slavery in Mexico, resulted in the state being created.

A small antigovernment faction emerged in the late 1990s, not unlike those in Chiapas. This faction demanded more local control and independence from Mexico. At present, its influence has been small, and the Mexican army has contained the faction's forces. Time will tell if this newest move for independence will be resurrected.

The area known now as Oaxaca was home to many local tribes thousands of years ago, building such archeological wonders as Monte Albán, Mitla, and Yagul. At first the Zapotec and Miztec civilizations ruled this area. When the Aztecs invaded in the 15th century they absorbed the other tribes and gave Oaxaca its name. In the Nahuatl language, Oaxaca means "by the acacia grove."

When the Spanish invaded, Oaxaca fell to the conquistadors. As a reward, the Spanish king gave Cortés the official title of Marquis of the Oaxaca Valley. Cortés never settled in the area, but until the early 1900s his descendants held title to the land.

In the 20th century, Oaxaca has been prominent in politics. Two presidents have come from this area—Benito Juárez, the first full-blooded Indian to become a head of state, and Porfirio Díaz, who ruled Mexico for more than 30 years. Díaz constructed railways and encouraged modernization, but he was removed from power in 1911, when revolutionaries plunged the country into civil war.

Since then Oaxaca has struggled to maintain its infrastructure and to improve itself. To help the state achieve this goal, the government has made massive investments in the tourist industry on the coastline.

A colorful display of fresh fruit at Mercado Central, the bustling main market of Acapulco.

3

THE ECONOMY

The Pacific South, like much of Mexico, is very poor. However, rich natural resources and growing industries provide hope for the future.

Over the years Colima has developed a reputation as a leading producer of lemons, providing more than 60 percent of the domestic market. Bananas and coconuts are close behind, as well as corn, rice, and mangos. Constant improvements to the land through techniques such as irrigation will increase production of these popular foods. Other industries have also moved in, such as processing plants for cotton, rice, and corn (maize), as well as salt refining and manufacturing leather goods. Beverage production and clothing production are also major industries. As a result, the manufacturing industry has over 600 industrial plants in this rather small state. The recent discovery of iron ore has encouraged the development of processing plants, with the result that Colima is now one of Mexico's largest iron-producing states. The port of Manzanillo, which handles both domestic and international shipping, has gained major importance as a hub for trade with the United States and the countries of Central and South America, as well as countries across the Pacific Ocean.

On the coastline, the tourism industry has taken a firm hold, with Manzanillo welcoming thousands of visitors each year to its white sandy beaches and wonderful fishing. Around these beaches has sprung up many businesses to entertain and enthrall visitors to this vibrant part of Colima. Two major modern international airports, as well as over 118 miles (190 kilometers) of railways, make this a thriving area. With a total population of just under 450,000, Colima has plenty of room to grow and develop in the future.

Chiapas is a leading national producer of coffee, but it also produces rubber, *cacao*, and cattle. The state has valuable mineral resources as well, with major sources of silver, gold, and copper that remain untapped, while petroleum production has begun in earnest. The Grijalva River is also a main producer of hydroelectric power, serving the growth and expansion of industries in the area. Thirty percent of all of Mexico's hydrological resources are in Chiapas, with its three dams generating 58 percent of the hydroelectricity output and 2.2 percent of the nation's total electricity production. This makes it a vital part of the revitalization of Mexico and of the Chiapas region. With four airports and several large airfields, as well as over 8,700 miles (14,000 kilometers) of highways and railways, Chiapas is poised to become a vital trading partner not for only the United States but also for the rest of Latin America.

Due to the growth of interest in its Mayan ruins, Chiapas has begun to develop a large tourist base using the Mundo Maya travel circuit. A program designed by the Mexican government, its intention is to showcase the Mayan ruins and create the infrastructure needed to

Three women lace shoes at a shoe factory. Colima and Oaxaca are known for their production of leather goods such as shoes.

accommodate the many tourists who want to visit and admire these ancient ruins deep in the Lacandon jungle. An unfortunate side effect of this development is that with the jungle being cut back for development and the trees burnt off for cattle grazing, the original inhabitants of these areas are being forced to move away from their ancestral lands.

Guerrero's strength lies primarily in its tourist industry, with Acapulco famous worldwide for its hot and sunny beaches. With two international airports and over 4,970 miles (8,000 kilometers) of highways and roads, easy access is available to both tourists and to manufacturers.

Acapulco is only part of a major tourist development strategy in Mexico, however. Taxco, a small colonial town known for its silver; Ixtapa; and Zihuatanejo all provide most of the same tourist attractions as Acapulco, but at a slower pace.

While tourism is a major part of Guerrero's economy, other industries are beginning to come to the forefront as the overall

A woman picks shade-grown coffee beans on her father's farm in northern Oaxaca. Coffee is one of the major export crops of both Chiapas and Oaxaca.

Mexican economy improves and allows new expansion and innovations. Metallurgy, or working with gold and silver, has taken an important role in the revitalization of the area, as the reputation of Taxco silver rises around the world. The local resources of silver and gold mean that the talented artisans in the area already have easy access to supplies. Other industries present in the state include food and coffee processing. With the tropical climate, it is hard to grow crops, so Guerrero depends more on its natural resources rather than agriculture.

The major economic industry in Oaxaca is agriculture, with the state leading all others in coffee production. Sugarcane and tobacco

are also common crops, with cattle raising and fruit orchards plentiful in the area.

The fertile ground offers up good harvests, but it also hides a great wealth of mineral deposits, especially coal and iron. Major deposits of marble and granite can be found specifically on the isthmus, and *graphite*, *mica*, and *uranium* are scattered throughout the state. Unfortunately, many of these resources are not yet being mined, but in the future, as Mexico continues to modernize its cities and industries, these minerals will be developed as well.

Three industrial areas on Oaxaca offer processing centers for the minerals that are being mined, as well as production of such items as cement and frozen foods. Two major areas of development by the government involve the soft drink industry and the manufacturing and exporting of high-quality reproductions of pre-Columbian jewelry.

A harvest of Mexican coconuts, one of the main crops of Colima.

Oaxaca is known worldwide for the hand-woven textiles and leather goods made by the local craftsmen. The pottery created by the residents is also popular in many countries, reminders of the ancient peoples who occupied this area for centuries.

With three international airports and a large harbor situated at Salina Cruz, Oaxaca offers easy access to the rest of the world and to their markets.

In January 1994, the North American Free Trade Agreement (NAFTA) went into effect between Mexico, Canada, and the United States. The agreement eliminates restrictions on the flow of goods, services, and investments, such as tariffs (taxes imposed by the government on imported goods). It allows free trade between the countries.

NAFTA has helped the *maquiladora* industry in the states of Mexico's Pacific South. A maquiladora is a Mexican factory that is allowed to import duty-free (without tax) the materials and equipment needed to produce goods. Most maquiladoras produce electronics, textiles, and auto parts and accessories.

Until recently, these states had no big industries. Instead, most factories were small businesses where silver jewelry or local clothing was made. The governments of these states have tried to attract bigger businesses, and in 1998 large plants were built for the production of foods such as chocolate and citrus fruit products. In the same year, the first maquiladoras were also built in this region, especially in the

The evening sun silhouettes an oil platform off the coast of Mexico. Industrial work has become a major source of income for skilled laborers.

COLIMA

Per capita income: 14,621 pesos

Natural resources: iron ore

GDP in thousands of pesos:
23,551,976

Percentage of GDP:
Manufacturing 11%
Commerce 50%
Service industries 39%

Exports: lemons, corn, rice, mangos, bananas, coconuts

GUERRERO

Per capita income: 7,573 pesos

Natural resources: Beautiful beaches to attract tourists.

GDP in thousands of pesos:
73,427,393

Percentage of GDP:
Manufacturing 15%
Commerce 48%
Service industries 36%
Other 1%

Exports: silver, gold

CHIAPAS

Per capita income: 6,123 pesos

Resources: silver, gold, copper, petroleum, hydroelectric power

GDP in thousands of pesos:
69,755,324

Percentage of GDP:
Manufacturing 12%
Commerce 55%
Service industries 33%

Exports: coffee, rubber, cacao, cattle

OAXACA

Per capita income: 6,172 pesos

Resources: coal, iron, marble, granite

GDP in thousands of pesos:
64,708,914

Percentage of GDP:
Manufacturing 17%
Commerce 47%
Service industries 36%

Exports: cement, frozen foods, textiles, leather goods, fruit, jewelry, coffee, soft drinks, tobacco, sugar cane

northern part of Guerrero. In one year, these helped to increase the state's export income by 30 percent. The region is hopeful that this positive trend will continue.

Recently, maquiladoras have caused international concern because of the unsafe and unfair working conditions that exist in many of these factories. Maquiladoras do help bring foreign investment to the states of the Pacific South, however.

PER CAPITA INCOME = the amount earned in an area divided by the total number of people living in that area
GDP = Gross Domestic Product, the total value of goods and services produced during the year
1 PESO = about $0.10, as of August 2008

Figures from INEGI, the Mexican National Institute of Statistics, based on Mexico's 2000 census.

This terracotta dog sculpture found in Colima was created approximately 1,500 years ago.

4

THE CULTURE

Colima, like many Mexican states, shares many holidays with other parts of the country. But some *fiestas* are specifically for certain churches or communities, and each year both the people of the region and tourists enjoy the celebration. Here is a list of the most popular festivals in the capital city of Colima.

✳ **Fiesta de la Virgen de la Salud**
January 23–February 2.
Centered in the northern part of town around Gallardo and Corregidora Avenues. Here you can find crafts, food, wonderful folk dancing and fireworks to go along with the parade.

✳ **Fiesta Charrotaurina**
February 7–23
In Villa de Álvarez, a few miles northwest of Colima City. Processions start from the Jardín de Libertad; leading to carnivals and festive displays; you might even see a bullfight as well.

* **Fiesta de San José**
March 9–19.
Centered on the west side near Quintero and Suárez, religious processions are common in this festival, along with a variety of local crafts and dancing for the tourist.

The *Casa de Cultura* of Colima also sponsors an annual fine arts festival in late November and early December. Everything from ballet to opera to painting will be on exhibit, displaying the best the area has to offer.

And if you visit Colima, be sure to pick up one of the most popular tourist items, a replica of the famous Colima Dog. Statues like this have been found throughout the area at various archeological sites. They have been reproduced many times over for the eager tourist looking for a novel souvenir.

A majority of the inhabitants of Chiapas are the descendants of the original Mayan tribes who lived there. For centuries, they have resisted outside control and demanded their part of the riches being reaped from the soil. As a result, constant turmoil between the local rebels and the Mexican government sometimes leads to armed conflict. When the average pay consists of only nine U.S. dollars a day, it's not hard to imagine the frustration and anger of the residents who look to the north and see the riches of the United States. Immigration is a major industry here as well, with many men leaving their families to try and work legally or illegally across the border. They do not believe the Mexican government's assurances that the economy will improve quickly so that they will not have to seek their fortunes elsewhere. As a result, many villages have very few men of working age, with a majority of the males being either too young

Zapatista rebels take a break in the Lacandona jungle near Chiapas in January 1994. The goal of the Zapatista Army for National Liberation is independence from Mexico for the state of Chiapas.

to leave or retired workers living on a meager (or nonexistent) *pension*.

The rebels are called the Zapatista Army for National Liberation, and their goal is the eventual independence of Chiapas. When Vicente Fox became president in 2000, he promised to listen to their complaints. Members of the army heard this message, and in March 2001, they marched to Mexico City and staged a large rally in favor of Indian rights, which came to be called the "Zapatour." Conflict between the Zapatistas and the Mexican government remains, but authorities now recognize that indigenous Mexicans need and want a political voice.

Despite their poverty and rebellion, the people of Chiapas still love to celebrate. Some of their major holidays include:

* **Chiapa de Corzo's San Sebastián Festival**
  January 15–23

* **Carnival and Easter Week in San Juan Chamula**
  Held every Friday during Lent, this festival includes the local villagers walking over hot coals!

* **Chamula's San Juan Festival**
  June 22–24

Townsfolk costumed as skeletons carry a coffin through the streets in a mock funeral during the Day of the Dead, which celebrates the souls of friends and family members who have passed away. Day of the Dead celebrations may appear strange to outsiders, but they carry a great deal of significance for Mexican participants.

✳ **Festival of the Patron Saint of San Cristóbal**
July 24–25
During this time brightly decorated trucks, buses, and cars parade up a hilltop to the San Christóbal Church for the celebration and ceremonies of this religious holiday.

✳ **Celebration of San Lorenzo in Zinacantán**
August 6–11

✳ **Día de los Muertos** (The Day of the Dead)
October 31–November 2
Celebrated throughout Mexico, this event includes festive grave-side celebrations and enchanting colorful costumes.

The Virgin Mary holds special religious meaning to devout Christian Mexicans. She is often called Our Lady of Guadalupe, because she appeared to a Mexican man in Guadalupe in 1531. During parades in her honor, the image of Mary is carried through the streets to the church built where she is believed to have appeared.

✳ **The Feast of the Virgin of Guadalupe**
December 12 (although in Tuxtla Gutiérrez, it's celebrated for an entire week!)

✳ **Día de la Mexicanidad**
September 14
Celebrated in every village and city in Chiapas, this holiday commemorates the independence of Chiapas from Guatemala and its entrance into Mexico as a state.

Many residents of Guerrero are descendants of the Olmecs, though their ancestors also came from a variety of other civilizations, including the Spanish. Today, many of these people make their living working in or around the hotels and the beaches. There the beautiful and creative arts and crafts of the Guerrero citizens can be seen and bought by any visitor. Many craft markets feature brightly colored masks and almost garishly painted wooden fish and ceramics, all reflecting the ancient culture of their makers.

Mexican actors play the roles of Jesus and a Roman soldier during a Holy Week festival. This reenacting of the crucifixion is one of the most symbolic and emotional rituals of the year for Christian Mexicans.

Like all the other Mexican states, the people of Guerrero love to celebrate. Here are some of their festivals:

✳ **The Feast of Santa Prisca and San Sebastián**
January 18–20
Held in Taxco, this celebration is for the town's patron saints with plenty of fireworks and music and parties.

✳ **Holy Week** (from Palm Sunday to Easter Sunday)

Much like the rest of Mexico, Guerrero holds this major Catholic event in high esteem; merging Christian and Indian traditions within the ceremonies. Images have a more Indian look to them as the local inhabitants use the ritual and the ceremony as a personal mirror to reflect their community.

✳ **Día de San Miguel** (Saint Michael's Day)
September 29
Dances and pilgrimages to churches celebrate this religious holiday.

✷ **Día del Jumil**
November 1–2
Following the Day of the Dead celebrations (throughout Mexico), the Taxco people will head for a nearby hill outside the city. Here they will capture the *jumiles*, crawling insects somewhat like ants or beetles, and eat them, either alive or cooked in a stew or a fried dish, usually with plenty of hot sauce. The jumil is said to taste like iodine but is considered a great treat by the local people who eagerly anticipate this holiday.

✷ **Jornadas Alarconianas**
The biggest celebration in Taxco, this festival honors one of Mexico's most famous writers with theater, dance and concerts rotating around this famous writer. Juan Ruiz de Alarcón y Mendoza was born in 1581 and died in 1639, but he is still famous for his plays and comedies. Born in Mexico, he studied law in Spain and became a member of the governing body for the Spanish colonies (including Mexico at the time) in 1626. The actual dates for this celebration vary each year, but the fiestas include Taxco's famous fireworks as well as music and dancing into the early hours of the morning. Popular with tourists and local inhabitants alike, this festival is a major yearly event.

In Oaxaca, a majority of the people are almost direct descendants of the native Zapotec and Miztec, who built such archeological wonders as Mitla and Monte Albán. The state's culture reflects these ancient civilizations. Brightly woven textiles and skillfully created jewelry and pottery attest to the influences of these long-ago people.

45

Two out of three Oaxaqueños (inhabitants of Oaxaca) can trace their lineage back to the Zapotec and Miztec cultures. However, they speak 16 different languages and over 50 individual dialects. To many of these people, Spanish is a second language if it is learned at all. Oaxaca has one of the highest native populations in all of Mexico.

Due to the influence of the Spanish invaders, the majority of the people are Roman Catholic, with very few Protestants. The church and monastery of Santo Domingo, located in Oaxaca City itself, is a national monument drawing tourists and local worshippers alike to the classical architecture. As with many other states in Mexico, some holidays combine the feast days of Catholic saints with native religious elements.

✳ The Day of the Dead
October 31–November 2
As in the rest of the country, Oaxaqueños celebrate this holiday by visiting graveyards and holding celebrations. These often involve whole families having picnics in the cemeteries with the favorite food of the deceased. Many villages have large parties; the most popular of these is in Xoxo, but the celebrations in Atzompa and Xochimilco are well known as well. The festivals and parties are open to everyone, and tourists are welcome.

✳ Noche de Rábanos (Night of the Radishes)
December 23
For this celebration the local market is transformed into a wonderful art display as local growers and artists display their radish crops

and creations. With sculptures ranging from Nativity displays to the Space Shuttle, the artistic competition is judged not only on the complexity but also on the size and quality of the radishes. Other creations involve dried flowers and cornhusks.

✳ **Guelaguetza** (Zapotec for "offering" or "gift")
Held the last two Mondays each July, this is a major state celebration that takes place in Oaxaca City. Dancers from all the cities and villages meet in Oaxaca City, bringing the best their area has to offer, from coffee to fruit and everything in between. Meeting at the Guelaguetza Auditorium; dancers perform complicated and elaborate dances for an entire day in the open spaces of the auditorium. Wearing authentic costumes handed down throughout the years, they recreate the feeling of their ancestors who also celebrated the wealth of their territory.

Throughout the Pacific South, celebrations brighten the lives of the people who live there. These colorful fiestas attract tourists to the wonderful culture of this area.

	STATE POPULATION	GROWTH RATE
Chiapas	3,920,892	2.0%
Colima	542,627	2.4%
Guerrero	3,079,649	1.6%
Oaxaca	3,438,765	1.3%

Mexico's ethnic groups
Indian-Spanish (mestizo): 60%
Indian: 30%
White: 9%
Other: 1%

Education 12 years of education is required from ages 6 through 18. About 94% of school-age children are enrolled in school. The literacy rate is 91%.

Mexico's religions
Roman Catholic: 77%
Protestant: 6%
Unspecified or none: 17%

This relief sculpture in Michoacán shows the conquistador Gonzalo de Sandoval receiving a gift from the king of Colima in 1521.

5

THE CITIES AND COMMUNITIES

Colima's capital city is also called Colima. Almost exactly in the center of the triangle-shaped state, it is also known as "The City of the Palm Trees" due to the wonderful vegetation around and inside the city. With approximately 160,000 inhabitants, Colima has many wonderful tourist attractions, from the Zócalo (Main Square) with its beautiful trees and architecture, to the Cathedral (finished in 1824), to the many museums displaying ancient art, musical instruments, and ceremonial masks.

Walking into Colima's center you'll find a variety of places to visit: from the Jardín de Libertad (Garden of Liberty) where you can find stores carrying anything and everything, to the Museo de Historia (Museum of History) where you can view wonderfully preserved pre-Columbian pottery. Connected by highway to Guadalajara, this capital city boasts a wonderful variety of Mexican foods, as well as a large and recognized university.

Perched on the Pacific Coast is Manzanillo, the main port of Colima. In 1522, Gonzalo de Sandoval dropped anchor just north of Manzanillo Bay in the Bay of Salagua. He was searching for safe sites for travelers to land and venture ashore, but he moved onward into the center of Colima, leaving the bay behind. It wasn't until 1527 that Manzanillo Bay was fully explored by navigator Álvaro de Saavedra. First named Santiago's Bay of Good Hope, it soon became a popular site for expeditions both arriving and leaving through the not-so-safe waters. Pirates swept up and down the Pacific Coast at this time, seeking treasure and finding it in the *galleons* that left Santiago's Bay loaded with gold, silver, and copper.

In 1825, the port of Manzanillo, named after the numerous groves of *manzanillo* trees that flourished on the shore, was officially opened. Over the years the importance of the seaport grew. In 1915, it was declared the state capital when Pancho Villa's troops threatened to capture the city of Colima.

Thanks to a major renovation a few years ago, the harbor has become accessible to all major shipping lines and their vessels. This has helped the city to grow even more, and brought more visitors. Tourists can fish or take advantage of the many wonderful beaches that line the coast. Manzanillo also boasts many other attractions, among them a *mural* done by local artist Jorge Chávez Carrillo and the University Museum of Archaeology.

Further down the coast from Manzarillo is Tecomán, one of the most popular coastal towns. Famous for its seafood, the restaurants here offer more than the usual choices. On the menu you can find shellfish soup and

A bird's-eye view of Manzanillo, the main port of Colima and one of the state's most important cities.

octopus. A nearby favorite fishing spot is the Amela Lagoon, located just one hour from Tecomán on the main highway. Here the avid fisherman can enjoy one of the best fishing experiences possible anywhere.

Coquimatlán lies just west of Colima and offers the visitor an old-fashioned atmosphere with cobbled streets far from the hustle and bustle of the big city. Each year this city is witness to the most traditional religious celebration in the entire state—the carrying of the "Señor de la Expiración" (Lord of the Expiration) from the Church of San Pedro inside Coquimatlán to the nearby town of Rancho de Villa. Held on the first Tuesday of every January, it features street dances and fairs.

And if you want to get a closer look at volcanoes, there is no better place than the Nevado de Colima National Park, right at the

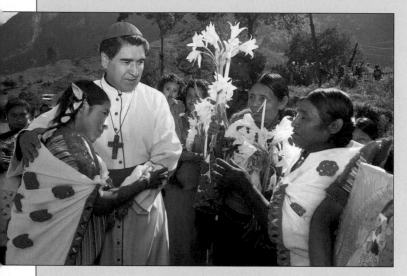

The bishop of San Cristóbal de las Casas, in Chiapas, is greeted by Tzotzil Indians and mestizos before a procession to San Pedro Church in Arizmendi.

northeast edge of the state. Ideal for mountaineering and camping, you may also have the opportunity to venture close to Volcán de Fuego, an active volcano.

San Cristóbal de las Casas is still one of Chiapas' main cities, although no longer the capital. Near the center of the state, this ancient city offers many attractions to the average tourist, not least of which is the charming atmosphere. Tourists feel as though they travel back in time at the many craft shops and stores. With a population of approximately 150,000, the city sits at an altitude of 6,888 feet (2,100 meters) above sea level and offers a central hub for tourists traveling to the archeological sites nearby.

In 1892, Tuxtla Gutiérrez replaced San Cristóbal as the capital city of Chiapas. With a thriving population of 390,000, this city is rapidly transforming its historical buildings and ancient homes to a thriving metropolitan center as it moves forward into the 21st century. It is home to one of the most innovative zoos in the world, the Miguel Álvarez del Toro Zoo (also known as ZooMAT). Here all the animals are native to Chiapas and Mexico, and all run free in their natural habitat for visitors to watch and admire. Botanical gardens and museums also help make Tuxtla Gutiérrez a worthwhile destination for any tourist. Not too far from the city are the Mayan ruins of Bonampak and Yaxchilán, offering visitors a wonderful archeological experience.

Acapulco is one of the best known cites of Guerrero, if not Mexico itself. Originally used as a major port for the Spanish to ferry their treasures from their conquests around the world, this city has become world renowned for its beaches and tourist industry.

Taxco is one of the smaller but still popular cities, situated at the foothills of the Sierra Madre. Famous for their silverware, the skilled

The beaches of southwestern Mexico are a great draw for tourists. One of the most popular destinations is Acapulco, Guerrero, where luxury hotels overlook the white sands and clear waters.

artisans of this city are descended from the original immigrants who came here centuries ago to search for silver. After the original silver rush in the 1500s, interest tapered off in this area due to low silver levels—until the 1700s, when a Frenchman discovered a thick rich vein that revitalized the silver industry and boosted the local economy once again. But it was an American, William G. Spratling from New Orleans, who really set Taxco's wheels in motion. Falling quickly in love with Taxco, he set up a shop and began to produce silver jewelry based on pre-Columbian designs and artwork. He drew in local townsfolk as his *apprentices*, and soon his work earned Taxco worldwide recognition and fame. Many of his descendants and their apprentices carry on this rich tradition to this day.

Chilpancingo, the capital city of Guerrero, is approximately 80 miles (130 kilometers) from Acapulco near the center of the state. With a population of 97,000, this city is also known as Chilpancingo de los Bravos. The extended name honors its local heroes in the war against Spain, three brothers, the most famous of whom was Nicolás Bravo. The city serves as the regional center for the agricultural products grown in the area.

Like Acapulco, Ixtapa and Zihuatanejo attract tourists, but they are much less built up and modernized. Offering a quieter, gentler atmosphere, these two towns have sports fishing and an abundance of restaurants and hotels. They cater to the visitor who is looking for a relaxing visit to Mexico.

Oaxaca City, in the state of Oaxaca, lies in a valley surrounded by low mountains, near the center of the state. Its full name is Oaxaca de Juárez, in honor of President Benito Juárez. According to Aztec folklore, the city's original name was Huaxyacac, and it was founded in 1486, during the time that the Aztecs ruled over the Miztecs and Zapotecs. Active in the Mexican Revolution against Spain and later in the resistance against the French, this city is famous for its hand-wrought gold and silver as well as its artisans' handicrafts and artwork. Unfortunately, the city has suffered damage from ongoing earthquakes.

Monte Albán, a short daytrip away from Oaxaca, is one of the state's treasures. Overlooking the Oaxaca Valley at 1,300 feet (396 meters), this city is well over a thousand years old and provides glimpses of the Zapotec culture.

Mitla lies just southeast of Oaxaca, and its history is much like Monte Albán's. But what makes this city interesting for scholars are the strange geometric patterns found everywhere. The designs contain not a single image of a person nor any depiction of events; they are nothing but abstract designs carved into brilliant stones. The name comes from the Aztec word "mictlán" or "place of the dead."

Taxco, located in the Sierra Madres, is an important city in Guerrero.

CHRONOLOGY

3000 B.C.	Olmecs live in what is now Guerrero.
200 B.C.–A.D. 900	The Maya settle in Oaxaca and Chiapas.
1200s	Monte Albán becomes part of the Miztec culture; Mitla as well is settled and the vast murals are produced making it unlike any other city in the world.
1420–1500	Aztecs take over the center of the Mexican Valley and begin to expand their empire. Eventually they rule most of Mexico, dominating the culture and the other native people still present.
1517	The Spanish arrive in Mexico. Chiapas becomes a part of Guatemala under the Conquistadors.
1523	Colima City founded.
1810–1821	Mexican War of Independence is fought against Spain.
1824	Chiapas gains independence from Guatemala and joins Mexico as a free state.
1829	President Vicente Guerrero abolishes slavery in Mexico; years before the United States.
1849	State of Guerrero created from land taken from other nearby states.
1858	Benito Juárez, originally from Oaxaca, becomes president of Mexico.
1877	Porfirio Díaz, also of Oaxaca, takes control of the government.

1880   Railroad built across Colima from Capital City to Manzanillo by Porfirio Díaz, enabling transportation of materials both into and out of the interior.

1892   The capital of Chiapas moved from San Cristóbal to Tuxtla Gutiérrez.

1910–1917   Major damage done to the Colima area in the Mexican Revolution.

1974   Discovery of major crude petroleum deposits in Chiapas with further exploration and development following.

1993   President Carlos Salinas de Gortari signs the North American Free Trade Agreement (NAFTA) with United States President George Bush.

1994   Violence breaks out in Chiapas from Zapista rebels who want independence.

2000   Vicente Fox is elected president.

2001   Promising reforms, Fox's government holds discussions with the Zapatistas as well as other rebel factions.

2002   Latin American leaders, including Mexico's Vicente Fox, meet in Argentina for the Global Alumni Conference to discuss technological and economic issues.

2003   A 7.6-magnitude earthquake kills 29 people and leaves thousands homeless, mostly in the state of Colima.

2006   In Oaxaca City, a teacher's strike turns into seven months of protests against state governor Ulises Ruiz, resulting in at least 18 deaths; Felipe Calderón becomes president of Mexico.

2008   The Mexican government pledges $42 million to improve sanitation and curb pollution in tourist-heavy Acapulco.

FOR MORE INFORMATION

CHIAPAS

Government of Chiapas
www.chiapas.gob.mx

State Tourism Office
Blvd. Belisario Dominguez No. 950
Planta Baja
CP 29060 Tuxtla Gutiérrez, Chis.
Tel: (961) 61-7-05-50
E-mail: st@turismochiapas.gob.mx

COLIMA

Government of Colima
www.colima.gob.mx

State Tourism Office
Portal Hidalgo No. 96 Centro
CP 28000 Colima, Col.
Tel: (312) 312-2857
Fax: (312) 312-8360
E-mail: turiscol@palmera.
  colimanet.com

GUERRERO

Government of Guerrero
www.guerrero.gob.mx

State Tourism Office
Av. Costera Miguel Alemán No. 4455
Centro Cultural y de Convenciones
de Acapulco
Fracc. Club Deportivo
CP 39850 Acapulco, Gro.
Tel: (744) 484-4416
Fax: (744) 481-4583
E-mail: info@sectur.guerrero.gob.mx

OAXACA

Government of Oaxaca
www.oaxaca.gob.mx

State Tourism Office
Independencia No. 607 esq.
García Vigil
CP 68000 Oaxaca, Oax.
Tel: (951) 516-0717
Fax: (951) 516-1500
E-mail: info@oaxaca.gob.mx

THINGS TO DO AND SEE

COLIMA

Fuego de Colima and Volcán de Fuego, an active volcano

Fishing in Manzanillo

CHIAPAS

San Cristóbal's historical sites

Huixtán and Oxchuc, two small villages known for the exquisite colors of their embroidery

Palenque, an ancient Mayan site

GUERRERO

The Cacahuamilpa caverns

The cliff divers of La Quebrada in Acapulco

The underwater shrine just south of the Peninsula de las Playas, a submerged bronze statue of the Virgin of Guadalupe

OAXACA

The popular archeological sites and museum at Monte Albán

The resort at Huatulco, a government project to encourage tourism

Resort attractions at Puerto Escondido

GLOSSARY

Apprentices	Students who train under an expert.
Asset	Resource or benefit.
Cacao	The bean used to make chocolate.
Conquistadors	Spanish conquerors of the New World.
Dyewoods	Wood used for making dyes.
Fiestas	Spanish parties or celebrations.
Galleons	Heavy, square-rigged sailing ships used in the 15th to the early 18th centuries, especially by the Spanish.
Graphite	A soft black form of carbon used to make lead pencils, electrolytic anodes, and nuclear reactors.
Infrastructure	A country's public works, such as roads, railroads, and schools.
Mahogany	A reddish-brown hard wood from a tropical tree.
Malaria	A disease caused by one-celled parasites; spread to humans by mosquitoes.
Manzanillo	A small apple.
Mica	A mineral that can be separated into very thin, transparent layers.
Mural	A large picture painted on a wall.
Pension	Money paid by the government or a business to a person after retirement.
Plateau	High, flat land.
Rosewood	The reddish wood from a tropical tree.
Smallpox	A contagious disease that causes high fevers and pus-filled sores that leave deep scars.
Uranium	A heavy, silvery, radioactive element.

FURTHER READING

Chávez, Alicia Hernández. *Mexico: A Brief History*. Berkeley: University of California Press, 2006.

Coe, Michael D., and Rex Koontz. *Mexico: From the Olmecs to the Aztecs*. New York: Thames and Hudson, 2008.

Foster, Lynn V. *A Brief History of Mexico*. New York: Checkmark Books, 2007.

Franz, Carl, et al. *The People's Guide to Mexico*. Berkeley, Calif.: Avalon Travel Publishing, 2006.

Hamnet, Brian R. *A Concise History of Mexico*. New York: Cambridge University Press, 2006.

Joseph, Gilbert M., editor. *The Mexico Reader: History, Culture, Politics*. Durham, N.C.: Duke University Press, 2002.

Meyer, Michael C., et al. *The Course of Mexican History*. New York: Oxford University Press, 2002.

INTERNET RESOURCES

Mesoweb
http://www.mesoweb.com/welcome.html#externalresources

Mexico for Kids
http://www.elbalero.gob.mx/index_kids.html

Mexico Channel
http://www.mexicochannel.net

Publisher's Note: The websites listed on this page were active at the time of publication. The publisher is not responsible for websites that have changed their address or discontinued operation since the date of publication. The publisher reviews and updates the websites each time the book is reprinted.

61

INDEX

63

PICTURE CREDITS

CONTRIBUTORS

Roger E. Hernández is the most widely syndicated columnist writing on Hispanic issues in the United States. His weekly column, distributed by King Features, appears in some 40 newspapers across the country, including the *Washington Post*, *Los Angeles Daily News*, *Dallas Morning News*, *Arizona Republic*, *Rocky Mountain News* in Denver, *El Paso Times*, and *Hartford Courant*. He is also the author of *Cubans in America*, an illustrated history of the Cuban presence in what is now the United States, from the early colonists in 16th-century Florida to today's Castro-era exiles. The book was designed to accompany a PBS documentary of the same title.

Hernández's articles and essays have been published in the *New York Times*, *New Jersey Monthly*, *Reader's Digest*, and *Vista Magazine*; he is a frequent guest on television and radio political talk shows, and often travels the country to lecture on his topic of expertise. Currently, he is teaching journalism and English composition at the New Jersey Institute of Technology in Newark, where he holds the position of writer-in-residence. He is also a member of the adjunct faculty at Rutgers University.

Hernández left Cuba with his parents at the age of nine. After living in Spain for a year, the family settled in Union City, New Jersey, where Hernández grew up. He attended Rutgers University, where he earned a BA in Journalism in 1977; after graduation, he worked in television news before moving to print journalism in 1983. He lives with his wife and two children in Upper Montclair, New Jersey.

Sheryl Nantus lives in Brownsville, Pennsylvania, with her husband Martin and two cats. A Canadian and cervical cancer survivor, she enjoys cross stitch, computer gaming, and being a wonderful aunt to her niece Robyn and nephew Richard while extolling the virtues of hockey, lacrosse, and a good cup of tea to her American friends.

Pub